D0197857

It is Often Said

Comments and Comparisons of Traditional Christian Theology and Hebraic Thought

It is Often Said

Comments and Comparisons of Traditional Christian Theology and Hebraic Thought

By Tim Hegg

From a series of articles first published in *Bikurei Tziyon* magazine

FIRST FRUITS OF
ZION

Strengthening the love and appreciation
of the Body of Messiah for the Land,
the People and the Scriptures of Israel

First Fruits of Zion • *Bikurei Tziyon*
Israel • United States

Cover Design: Avner Wolff

First Edition
Printed in the United States of America

ISBN 1-892124-04-1

US Distribution Office
First Fruits of Zion
PO Box 620099
Littleton, Colorado 80162-0099 USA
Phone (303) 933-2119 or (800) 775-4807
Fax (303) 933-0997
www.ffoz.org

Additional Study Resources
Torah Club, a monthly Torah Study Course
HaYesod, a 14 week Hebraic Study Course
Bikurei Tziyon Magazine
Ascend Magazine

Other Books by Tim Hegg
The Letter Writer
ISBN 1-892124-16-5

For additional information, please visit http://www.ffoz.org

Contents

Preface

Shalom! Thank you for purchasing *It is Often Said*. Several years ago I asked Tim Hegg to write a series of articles from the perspective of Hebraic thought and theology that would address specific and common Christian misunderstandings of Scripture. Thankfully Tim agreed. As a result I am pleased to present this journal of compiled articles that first appeared in *Bikurei Tziyon* magazine.

There is a challenge before all of us who choose to live a life submitted to God's Word as we understand it; for it is our sole source of authority on how we as believers are to behave. Predominant Christian theology claims that the Torah has no relevance in the lives of the Redeemed because it has been done away with. We believe quite the opposite, and it is our aim to explain from the Scriptures why the Torah still stands as a firm and solid foundation of holiness and godliness for all believers who call on the name of Jesus. I invite you to read the following chapters without prejudice to allow history and Scripture to speak for themselves.

We need to understand the nature and work of Christ on behalf of all who would believe and be called according to His purpose. Ephesians 2:8–9 states it best, "For by grace you have been saved through faith; and that not of yourselves, it is the gift of God; not as a result of works, so that no one may boast."

- Not by works
- Not under the Law
- Not by our own merit
- Not through our own righteousness

Until we know and understand that He has sought us out and called us by His Name, and this through no merit of our own, we are not ready to open the Torah. Only the solid stamp of God's grace will protect us from the tendency toward legalism (i.e., obeying

Torah as a means by which to gain or secure favor with God). It is only His grace that ensures our obedience is motivated by our love and thankfulness for what He has provided for us in and through His Son—Jesus Christ.

FFOZ has produced several other resources that focus on the Jesus-centric, Torah-based life of God's Redeemed, and includes a quarterly periodical entitled *Ascend*. The purpose of *Ascend* Magazine is:

> The driving force behind *Ascend* Magazine is a deep desire to strengthen Christian values by helping believers reconnect with the Hebrew roots of the faith. We believe that a Hebraic perspective on the Scriptures is essential to a proper understanding of Jesus' teaching and a full appreciation of what it means to be His disciples. *Ascend* voices a call to the body of Christ to rededicate our lives to being faithful servants of God. We believe this can only be done by recovering a Scripture-based lifestyle and restoring our faith to its original, intended dimensions.

Ascend's purpose is to deal with matters of the Torah in a way that many will see God's love, mercy and grace in the whole of His revelation to man—His Scriptures. We hope this publication proves to be a powerful tool in the Father's hand to bring a greater knowledge and understanding of the Torah, the Written and the Living; resulting in increased unity and application of the Scriptures in the Body of Christ.

Please contact our Colorado office for more information about this publication, and ask for our *1-800-4-YESHUA* Resource Guide, for more materials to assist you in your studies of the Hebraic roots of your faith.

Boaz Michael
Founder, First Fruits of Zion
www.ffoz.org
www.ascendmagazine.com

Foreword

Two thousand years of anti-Torah teachings and theologies have lulled many of us in the Body of Christ to sleep, and kept us from partaking of the rich, nourishing root of our ancient Hebraic faith. As a result of misguided teaching about the authority of the "Old Testament" for our lives, we find ourselves hungry and longing for direction and purpose, seeking the simplicity of a life of faith in Israel's Messiah.

There is an inherent contradiction in Christian theology which teaches an "Old Testament" morality, yet at the same time, when questioned about the validity of the Torah, claims that "Christ abolished the oldness of the letter" so that we would be free to walk in the "newness of the Spirit." By spurning the very source and foundation for their own moral instructions, Christian theologies are left standing in the air.

Numbers 15:16 says, "There is to be one law (Hebrew = "Torah") and one ordinance for you and for the alien who sojourns with you." Yet this is not what we see today. God's Torah has been divided into civil, moral, and ceremonial laws. Once the Torah is dissected in this way, it is subjected to the "pick and choose" notions of man, determining at will what believers in Christ are to obey and what they should dismiss as merely cultural or even legalistic. This has resulted in a faith that is skewed, unbalanced, and confusing both to believers and the world that watches. Is the Written Word, like the Incarnate Word, the same yesterday, today, and forever? Has the eternal, inspired Word of God really changed? Are not all of God's truths unchanging, and therefore applicable for all of His people throughout all of the ages?

This booklet specifically addresses and answers some of the common anti-Torah arguments so often heard in our times. It is our desire to provoke, challenge, and encourage believers to embrace the heritage and portrait of righteousness that has been kept from them for so long. By following in the footsteps of Christ as He modeled the life of Torah, we strive to strip away centuries of tradition, superstition, and teachings of man. Confronted by the simplicity of righteousness as it is revealed in God's Torah, both written and Living, we desire to return to a life of faith that honors our Father both in individuals and community, now and for the next generation as well.

A few of the main purposes of the Torah are: (1) to convict of sin and instruct in righteousness (Romans 7:7; 1John 3:4); (2) to reveal Christ to us individually (Luke 24:25-27; John 5: 46; Romans 10:1-13; Deuteronomy 18:15), and thus to teach us to walk as He walked; (3) to reveal the righteousness of God in Christ. When the Torah is lived out, it paints a true picture of Jesus for those outside the community of believers to see (1Corinthians 11:1; 1Peter 2:21).

By addressing these questions about the Torah and its place in the Christian's life, we hope to awaken in the hearts of the Redeemed the reality of their relationship with the Land, the People and the Scriptures of Israel. For thousands of years the Church has taught that it replaced Israel as the chosen people of God. Paul, however, says quite the opposite. In Romans, he reminds Gentile believers that they, "...being a wild olive, were grafted in among them and became partaker with them of the rich root of the olive tree," and warns against arrogance "toward the branches" (Romans 11:17, 18).

"Remember that you were at that time separated from Christ, excluded from the commonwealth of Israel, and strangers to the covenants of (the) promise, having no hope and without God in the world. But now in Christ Jesus you who formerly were far off have been brought near by the blood of Christ" (Ephesians 2:12, 13).

We cannot continue to walk in pride, opposed to our roots. The gospel was given to Israel to share with the nations, and through Christ those from the nations are grafted into Israel, through whom salvation and blessing are promised. It was never God's intention for the redeemed of the nations to remain separate from Israel and her Messiah.

The purpose of this book is to seek biblical answers for questions that are often raised when the idea of Torah life is contemplated. The Torah is a tree of life to those who have faith in Jesus (Psalm 19:7), for through Him we are dead to the condemnation of the Torah and are free to walk in a joyful life of obedience because of our love for God and our desire to do what is pleasing to Him. May the mercy, justice, righteousness, patience, and love that God reveals about Himself through the written Word of His Torah be evident in these pages (cf. Exodus 34:6–7).

In God's economy, the Torah is the constitution which mitigates Israel's government. No one is above God's Torah because no one is above God. His word is the final authority, and even the king is not to transgress it.

Deuteronomy 17:18–20

It is often said

"Jesus Broke the Sabbath"

The issue of the Sabbath was not an early one. Nowhere in the New Testament do we find any indication that anyone questioned the validity of the Sabbath. There is not one argument between Jesus and His antagonists over the issue of whether the Sabbath is a day that God commanded to be set apart. If there were controversies over the Sabbath, they related to the man-made laws that had been added to the Torah commandment.

Part of the Creative Order

The Sabbath precedes Sinai. It is given in Genesis 2 as the day that God Himself set apart and blessed over all the other days. In fact, the issue of the manna and when it was to be gathered (Exodus 16) shows that the Sabbath was well in place before the giving of the Torah on Sinai. That it became the sign of the Mosaic Covenant (Exodus 31:14ff) is something subsequent to its place in Creation. This is why Jesus Himself states "the Sabbath was made for man, not man for the Sabbath" (Mark 2:27). Note carefully that He did not say that the Sabbath was made

15

for the Jews, but for "man" or "mankind." Thus Jesus teaches us that the Sabbath is a matter of the Creative order that governs all of mankind, not just Israel.

The Messiah's Teaching

Jesus never broke the Sabbath, though He was accused of doing so. However, Jesus did take exception with the many man-made laws that had caused the Sabbath to be a burden, even in His time. Jesus wanted to restore the true Torah teaching about Sabbath, that it was a day of joy and blessing, not one that only multiplied the expanding list of what one could not do.

So, Jesus' custom was to be in the synagogue on Sabbath (Luke 4:16). It is common in our modern times to hear the question, *"What Would Jesus Do?"* Here, then, is an obvious answer. If it were the custom of Jesus to be with the gathered people of God on the Sabbath, would it not make perfect sense to do what He did? And if we are His disciples, before we stop doing what He did, should we not expect a clear statement in Scripture to that effect? On what basis should we disregard the direct commandments of God and the clear example of His Son, Jesus?

But where is there any statement in Scripture telling us that God no longer wants us to keep the Sabbath day? Where has He withdrawn the wonderful gift of Sabbath which He gave to His children? Where is the teaching of Jesus for us, His disciples, saying that the Sabbath has been changed? There is none! Should we follow the 3rd and 4th century Church leaders who said that the command of God, one that carried the death penalty for its neglect (Exodus 31:14f; Numbers 15:32f) is no longer important? Would we say the same thing about any of the other commandments? Why are we so willing to dismiss the fourth commandment without any direct statement of Scripture to do so?

Moreover, why would Jesus, in speaking of the last days, tell us "pray that your flight not be... on the Sabbath" (Matthew 24: 20)? Would not He have known that the Sabbath would be done away with for the last-days Church? Why should the Sabbath be a concern for anyone in the last days? Obviously, Jesus never envisioned a time when the Sabbath would be suspended.

Not only do the Scriptures never hint at the Sabbath being abolished or changed, but on the contrary we have the clear and direct statement of Jesus Himself that until heaven and earth pass away, nothing in the Torah will be done away with. Matthew 5:17–20 states clearly that Jesus did not come to abolish the Torah and Prophets, but to fulfill them (make them viable, alive, real). The text goes on to admonish the disciples of Jesus both to do the commandments and teach others to do them if we want to be great in the Kingdom of God.

The Apostle Paul Concurs

Paul is not concerned whether a person is a Jew or Gentile (circumcised or not circumcised). What he is concerned about is that everyone keeps the commandments (ICorinthians 7:19). Does anyone really believe that Paul did not include the 4th commandment in what he calls "the commandments"?

Moreover, on what basis would someone argue that the Sabbath has been changed to Sunday? Usually the answer to this question is that by the death and resurrection of Jesus the Sabbath has been done away with. But if the eternal sacrifice of Jesus is the instrument by which the Sabbath is abolished, how is it that in the Millennium it is reinstated?

In Isaiah 56:3ff and 58:13ff, both of which are surely millennial passages, the Sabbath is clearly in force, not only for Israel, but for all the foreigners who attach themselves to Israel. How could Jesus abolish the Sabbath with His eternal sacrifice, yet have it reinstated in His millennial reign? If He abolished it, there must have been something wrong with it. Why then would it be reinstated in the Millennium? Reason this way: if it was clearly in place in the time of Jesus, and it will clearly be in place in the Millennium, on what basis has it been suspended in the interim? If God had intended that His straightforward commandment should, in a given era, be disregarded, then surely He would have made this clear. Yet, no such statement can be found in all of Scripture.

Paul also kept the Sabbath (Acts 17:2) and walked strictly according to the Torah (Acts 21:24). But some will say that in Romans 14 Paul speaks of the Sabbath as something that is non-essential and even irrelevant. But Romans 14 is not dealing with the Sabbath (the word Sabbath is not found in that context). It is most likely addressing the controversy over which day to celebrate the Festival of Weeks (Leviticus 23:15–16—an argument which was well established between the Pharisees and Sadducees of His day) or even, perhaps, over which days to set aside for fasting . The fact that Paul labels the whole debate as a matter of "opinion" (Romans 14:1) should alert us to the fact that he could not be talking about something clearly stated in the Scriptures, like the Sabbath command.

Furthermore, it is unthinkable that with such a passing statement Paul could abolish a Torah commandment that was one of the central issues of his day. And all without even the slightest hint of debate or backlash! If Paul had taught that the Sabbath was no longer viable, this would have been added to the offenses his opponents listed against him. Yet, Paul is never accused of such a teaching. The simple fact is that to read Romans 14 as abolishing the Sabbath is to read it entirely out of its historical and grammatical context.

The First Day of the Week

Some might suggest that in the New Testament the first day of the week is mentioned as the meeting day for the followers of Jesus. But an investigation shows that there are only two times in the whole of the New Testament (Acts 20:7–12 and 1Corinthians 16:1–3) where the first day of the week is highlighted for Jesus' followers, and in the second of these, there is no clear evidence that they even met together. In the first reference, the meeting is obviously after the end of the Sabbath (when the first day of the week begins from a Hebrew standpoint), going late into the night. It was the custom of the early followers of Jesus to gather together with the Gentiles after the Sabbath to celebrate their life in Jesus. The Gentiles would be finished with work. Remember, their masters were not worshipers of God and thus would not have honored the Sabbath by giving their slaves the day off. It was at this kind of a meeting that Eutychus, sitting in the window, fell to his death. In the other text that mentions the first day of the week, Paul is giving an admonition to the congregations to gather money for the relief of the believers in Jerusalem. Gathering money would not have been appropriate on the Sabbath, so a different day was chosen. But this never negated the obvious fact that they continued to meet on the Sabbath and to set it apart as unto the LORD. The New Testament, with a unified voice, shows that the Sabbath—not the first day of the week—was the day upon which the followers of Jesus gathered together in synagogues.

In the final analysis, then, the Scriptures are replete with clear indications (through numerous examples and direct commands) regarding the keeping of the Sabbath. What Scripture lacks is *any* clear statement to the effect that the Sabbath has been abolished. But why would God want to abolish something that He gave to His children for joy and gladness?!

"It's not in the New Testament!"

It is said that only what is found in the New Testament applies to believers today. The inevitable shift away from the synagogue, which occurred in the 2nd and 3rd century Church, unwittingly created a subtle yet real break with the Old Testament. Since the Torah, Prophets, and Writings were the Scriptures of the synagogue, and since the emerging Christian Church wanted to define herself as different from the synagogue and as a new entity, it was only natural that an emphasis would be placed upon the New Testament to the detriment of the Old Testament. Being placed in an inferior position, the established Scriptures (the Tanach) or the so-called "Old Testament" remained valuable for the Christian community only in so far as they reinforced the teachings of Jesus and the Apostles. Still, the emerging Christian Church considered the Hebrew Scriptures to be the Word of

God, and they were therefore retained in the "Christian Bible."

The modern Christian Church, however, has moved well beyond even the 3rd and 4th century Church, and adopted a practical hermeneutic which accepts only the New Testament as authoritative in the believer's life. Something specifically taught in the Old Testament, but not clearly repeated in the New Testament, is considered applicable for Israel only and not for the Church. So some within the Christian community might admit that the Sabbath remains for Jews, but that it does so only because there exists an eternal covenant with them of which the Sabbath is a sign.

Yet it is clear that the Sabbath commandment took in all who were within the community of Israel, not just the native born Jew or the proselyte. This is clearly taught in the Torah: *"...but the seventh day is a Sabbath of the LORD your God: you shall not do any work—you, your son or daughter, your male or female slave, or your cattle, or the stranger who is within your settlements."* In this regard also note Exodus 23:12; Deuteronomy 5:14; 31:12.

The Sinai Covenant

What is more, those who stood at Mt. Sinai and ratified the covenant included far more than Jews, for the text clearly states that a "mixed multitude" left Egypt: "And a mixed multitude also went up with them, along with flocks and herds, a very large number of livestock" (Exodus 12:38). No doubt, some Egyptians and even others of foreign nationality had come to believe in the God of Israel and had left with Israel in the great deliverance and redemption. As they stood at Mt. Sinai, they entered into the covenant. It would seem likely that the verses found in the Torah declaring one and the same law for the "native born and for the foreigner (stranger)" has this mixed multitude in mind (Exodus 12:49; Leviticus 24:22; Numbers 9:14; 15:29).

It is true that the Sinai covenant was made with the nation of Israel, and that it has national ramifications as well as individual. This is apparent from the fact that land is allocated to Israel (as a fulfillment of the Abrahamic covenant), and nationalistic items such as an army, kings, and a census are spoken of and laws given pertaining to each. But that this nationalistic character of the covenant also includes non-Israelites is clear, and extends to all who attach themselves to Israel through faith in her God. This is apparently Paul's emphasis when he describes Gentile believers as becoming part of the "commonwealth" of Israel (Ephesians 2:12-13), having been distant before, but now having been brought near. Moreover, Paul's ingrafting picture of Romans 11, and the clear emphasis upon Abraham as the father of all who believe (Romans 4:16), moves toward the idea that the Gentile believer in Jesus, like the God-fearer, has taken up "residence" within Israel (grafted into the same root) and therefore has the privilege of living within the divine precepts of the Torah just as the Jewish believer.

Some might argue that the lists of sins attributed to the Gentiles by someone like Paul (in Romans 1, for instance) does not include the breaking of Sabbath. To this several responses may be given. First, that the nations should abide by the Torah is the vision of the prophets for the last days. The full spread of the gospel did not occur until the coming of the Messiah and the sending of the Spirit, so the knowledge of the Torah was not widespread. Secondly, none of the lists confess to being exhaustive. Thirdly, the fact that the Scriptures clearly teach that the Torah condemns the sinner (whether Jew or Gentile, cf. Galatians 3:10, 13) means that the sinner is judged as a law-breaker. Being condemned by one's works (cf. Revelation 20:12, 13) would require a standard for what would be accepted and what would not—this standard is God's Torah, a Torah which condemns all who are not in Jesus. That the unbeliever is condemned by the Torah would indicate that he or she is condemned for breaking all of it, not just part of it (note James 2:10).

Such a perspective is in concert with the punishment put upon the nations for failure to keep the Festival of Tabernacles, a Sabbath to the LORD (Zechariah 14:17-19). These nations did not stand at Sinai, nor did they enter into the two-sided covenant between Israel and God. Yet they are held to the standard of the Torah. This being the case, one cannot argue that present day Gentiles are exempt from the Torah on the basis of covenant ratification, for if such were the case, the same would apply to Gentiles in any era. That it clearly does not is evident from the prophetic texts, which consistently portray righteous Gentiles as observing the Sabbaths given to Israel (Isaiah 56:1ff; 58:13, 14; 66:23).

Some might further argue that when believers are called to obey the commandments of God, the most important question to ask is, "which commandments apply to me?" And some would answer that certain commandments, like the Sabbath, are not applicable for the present day Church. That there are specific laws given for specific groups is obvious (male/female, king/servant, married/single), but to single the Sabbath out as given only to the Jews needs further substantiation. The other nine Words (Commandments) are clearly universal in scope— an argument from silence (that Sabbath is not mentioned by the Apostles as a direct commandment) is insufficient to consider it entirely sectarian in its application. For why would God include one sectarian commandment together with nine universal commandments?

Flawed Hermeneutics

Actually, this kind of hermeneutic is flawed. To say that only the New Testament are directly applicable to the believer presents a numbers of problems. The first and most obvious is that the Apostles seem to go out of their way to show that the Scriptures or the Word of God forms the standard for the disciple of Jesus, yet in the time of the Apostles, the New Testament, as we have come to know it, did not exist as Scripture. Evangelical scholars agree that the New Testament did not circulate as canonical texts until late in the 1st century CE at the earliest, and most likely, until the 2nd century. Though some of the Apostolic writings may have been received as Divine doctrine for the early

Messianic congregations, most often when the Scriptures are referred to, it is the Old Testament and nothing more. To say, then, that the Christian Church receives as Divine doctrine only what the Apostles wrote is essentially to write off the 1st century congregations of "The Way" as having little relevance for us in matters pertaining to our life of faith.

Secondly, the hermeneutic which receives only what is stated or restated in the New Testament as Divine doctrine cannot be sustained by the New Testament writings themselves. In Romans 1:32, for example, Paul presumes that everyone agrees that the death penalty is prescribed for homosexuality— he presumes this because it is "the ordinance of God," that is, because it is so stated in the Torah. For Paul, since it is so stated in the Torah, it is received as Divine direction for the believing community to which he writes.

Thirdly, a great many ethical and moral values which we consider foundational have their basis in the Old Testament, not in the New. Where in the writings of the Apostles do we find laws regarding abortion, pedophilia, cruelty to animals, bearing false witness in a court of law, bestiality, and cross-dressing to name of few?

Fourthly, if all that is necessary to live a fully sanctified life before the LORD is what is found from Matthew to Revelation (setting aside those portions of the Gospels which are directly spoken to a Jewish audience), is there really any essential need for the Old Testament? One hardly thinks so, and one might go so far as to say that Marcion (whose "canon" essentially consisted of only Paul's writings) was right to unburden us from the first two-thirds of the Bible. Would not our spiritual energies be best spent upon the "essentials" rather than upon that which, in the final analysis, is no longer needed? Of course, the modern Christian Church is not suggesting that we abandon the Old Testament, but it seems that in a practical way such a hermeneutic moves in that direction.

Finally...

If the Old Testament is only a relic of the past, an antique which adorns one's shelf, but has no practical use in one's life, is it really being received as the Word of God which lives and abides forever? And if it is only being used as a magnifying glass to investigate more closely the really important words of God (the New Testament), is it functioning as the two-edged sword the Apostles claim it to be?

The truth of the matter is clear: the Torah is a brilliant light illuminating our souls with God's truth and pointing us time and time again to Jesus. It is the foundation, the *Yesod*, of all of Scripture. And only as we know it, and live it, are the Scriptures as a whole understood as they should be.

Comments and Comparisons of Traditional Christian Theology and Hebraic Thought

1. "The most important question to ask when reading a verse like 1Corinthians 7:19 ("...what matters is keeping the commandments of God.") is, "which commandments am I accountable for?" The answer will be different for male & female, Jew and Gentile, married and single, etc. The same applies to all the verses in the New Testament which talk about 'commandments'".

Some might argue that when believers are called to obey the commandments of God, the most important question to ask is, "Which commandments apply to me?" And some would answer that certain commandments, like the Sabbath, are not applicable for the present day Church. That there are specific laws given for specific groups is obvious (male/female, king/servant, married/single), but to single the Sabbath out as given only to the Jews needs further substantiation. The other nine Words (Commandments) are clearly universal in scope—an argument from silence (that Sabbath is not mentioned by the Apostles as a direct commandment) is insufficient to consider it entirely sectarian in its application. For why would God include one sectarian commandment together with nine universal commandments?

2. "The Sabbath is a sign of the two-party covenant made between Israel and God. It therefore does not apply to Gentiles. The two parties of the covenant were God and Israel—the Gentiles were not ever part of this picture."

Those who stood at Mt. Sinai and ratified the covenant included far more than Jews, for Exodus 12:38 clearly states that a "mixed multitude" left Egypt. As they stood at Mt. Sinai, they entered into the covenant. It would seem likely that the verses found in the Torah declaring one and the same law for the "native born and for the foreigner (stranger)" has this mixed multitude in mind (Exodus 12:49; Leviticus 24:22; Numbers 9: 14; 15:29).

3. "To those who may have been conditioned as part of the Jewish community to keep the Sabbath, Paul's guidelines are given in Romans 14. These texts clearly state that Sabbath observance had a place before Christ came, but they no longer need to be a part of our observance."

Romans 14 is not dealing with the Sabbath (the word Sabbath is not found in that context). It is most likely addressing the controversy over which day to celebrate the Festival of Weeks (an argument which was well established between the Pharisees and Sadducees of His day) or even, perhaps, over which days to set aside for fasting. The fact that Paul labels the whole debate as a matter of "opinion" (verse 1) should alert us to the fact that he could not be talking about something clearly stated in the Scriptures, like the Sabbath command.

Study Questions
"Jesus Broke the Sabbath"

1. Why is it significant that the Sabbath is mentioned at the very beginning of the Bible (Genesis 2:2,3)? Why might it be important to realize that the Sabbath was given before the Torah was revealed at Sinai?

2. When the Torah was given at Sinai, the Sabbath was chosen as the sign of the covenant. Why was the Sabbath a fitting sign of the Torah as a covenant? Exodus 31:14ff; Ezekiel 20:12,20

3. Jesus' regular custom was to be in the synagogue on the Sabbath (Luke 4:16). What does this mean for us as we strive to be His disciples?

4. It is clear that Jesus did not intend to do away with the Torah (Matthew 5:17–21). What does this mean with regard to the Sabbath? In light of His words in Matthew 24:20, does it seem possible that He intended the day of rest to be changed to the first day of the week?

5. In the millennial reign of Jesus, the Sabbath once again will be observed by all of God's people (Isaiah 56:3ff; 58:13–14). If this is what will be in place during Jesus' earthly reign, what reasons could be given for why it would be changed to Sunday in our times?

6. Paul's practice was to observe the Sabbath (seventh day of the week) as a day set apart to God, not the first day of the week (Acts 17:2; 21:24). In light of his admonition to "Be imitators of me, just as I also am of Messiah" (1Corinthians 11:1), how should we consider his observance of the Sabbath as a model for us?

7. From the viewpoint of Scripture, can it be maintained that the Sabbath was made only for the Jews? Exodus 20:8–11; 23:12; Deuteronomy 5:14; 31:12; Mark 2:27

8. If the Sabbath is the sign of the covenant God made with Israel, how can it apply to non-Jewish believers? What is the relationship between Israel and the non-Jewish believers in Jesus? Ephesians 2:12–13; Romans 11

9. Some in our day are saying that the Old Testament is no longer authoritative since the New Testament has come. Is there biblical warrant for such a belief? When Paul wrote that the Scriptures were profitable for us (2Timothy 3:16), what Scriptures did he have in mind?

10. One would expect that if God intended one of the Ten Commandments to be dismissed, He would plainly tell us so. Is there any place in the Bible that instructs us to cease observing the Sabbath? How would you understand the Apostolic passages that speak of the "first day of the week" (Acts 20:7; 1Corinthians 16:2) or the "Lord's Day" (Revelation 1:10)? Is there any indication in these passages that there was a regular meeting of the believers that had replaced the Sabbath?

When God revealed Himself to us He gave us a legal code. He gave us laws. Yet they are more than just laws, they are actual pieces of Godliness. Each commandment is a small revelation of God. More than just a bunch of rules, the laws of Torah are a reflection of the Lawgiver.

Deuteronomy 5:24; 30:11–14
Romans 10:5–8

It is often said

"Torah is a Burden"

It is often said, "Even the Apostles admitted the Torah was a burden no one could bear!" This statement characterizes a common sentiment about the Torah—one based upon an equally common interpretation of Acts 15 and the Jerusalem Council.

Let us look again at Acts 15 and the decision of the Apostolic Council convened in Jerusalem. What was the issue at hand? What had brought about the need for the Council in the first place? And how should we interpret the apostles' decision? What does all this tell us about the place of the Torah among the early followers of Jesus?

The Core Issue at the Jerusalem Council

The opening verses of Acts 15 present a clear picture of the core issue confronting the Jerusalem Council:

> And some men came down from Judea and began teaching the brethren, "Unless you are circumcised according to the custom of Moses, you cannot be

saved." And when Paul and Barnabas had great dissension and debate with them, the brethren determined that Paul and Barnabas and certain others of them should go up to Jerusalem to the apostles and elders concerning this issue.[1]

The issue at hand was whether or not a non-Jewish person could become a covenant member with Israel and share in the blessings of the covenant. God had made the covenant of blessing with Israel and no other nation.[2] Most Jews in Paul's day believed that only Jews had a place in the world to come. A Gentile could secure a place in the afterlife only by becoming a Jewish proselyte (convert), made possible, according to the Rabbis, through a ritual based entirely upon their rules but with no foundation in the Torah.

Therefore, when men from Judea taught that "unless you are circumcised (undergo the ritual of a proselyte) according to the custom of Moses, you cannot be saved," they were simply applying the standard theology of their day. The Council was dealing with this question—If Israel had a place in the world to come, did Gentiles, therefore, need to submit to the contemporary man-made proselytizing ritual in order to secure eternal life, that is, be saved?

Nowhere does God's Word outline a ceremony for a Gentile to become a proselyte. In fact, the Torah quite specifically states that the resident non-Jew was to be received as just that—a non-Jewish person who had attached himself to Israel and to her God. If God expected the believing Gentile to become a Jew through some ritual of conversion, there would be no reason for a verse such as Numbers 15:16: "There is to be one Torah and one ordinance for you and for the alien who sojourns with you."[3]

In fact, God's sacred Scriptures prescribe no method for becoming a proselyte, thus revealing that the rabbinic matter of proselytizing was entirely man-made.

The issue was one of status. What qualified a person to be assured of a place in the world to come—ethnic status or faith? Which was essential for salvation, identification as a Jew or as being "in Messiah"? Paul and the other apostles at the Jerusalem Council unanimously agreed that one's ethnic status had no bearing whatsoever on one's salvation. The crux was faith, not ethnicity.

Is the Torah a Burden No One Can Bear?

The predominant interpretations of Acts 15, however, center not on the issue of how to receive Gentiles into the body of Christ, but on whether the Torah bore any relevance to their life of faith.

The opening words of the chapter clearly define the real issue. Furthermore, the apostles' language indicates their struggle with the dominant theology of their day. The manmade rules of the oral Torah had become so interwoven with the interpretation and application of the written Torah that in many cases the two had become indistinguishable.

In the first speech recorded in our chapter, Peter uses language that signals an important key to the interpretation of this passage. He reminds his audience that he, the first apostle sent to the Gentiles, had witnessed the outpouring of the Spirit upon them with no proselytising process. Then he says:

> "Now therefore why do you put God to the test by placing upon the neck of the disciples a yoke which neither our fathers nor we have been able to bear? But we believe that we are saved through the grace of the Lord Jesus, in the same way as they also are."[4]

Here Peter makes several important assertions that are key for understanding his words. First, note that he puts at odds the "yoke which neither our fathers nor we have been able to bear" with salvation through faith. The Gentiles had been saved and graced by God's presence—evidenced by the Spirit—as a matter of their faith, not because they had changed status from Gentile to Jew. In Peter's mind, the "yoke" that the Judean teachers desired to place upon them was contrary to salvation based upon God's grace.

But here is a crux for the proper interpretation of the passage: Would Peter have referred to the written Torah as a yoke that "neither our fathers nor we have been able to bear?" The common answer of Christian interpreters is a resounding "yes!" Taking the position that the Jews of his day believed their salvation was gained through obedience to the Torah, Peter's statement is interpreted as a ringing declaration against salvation by works.

But the Council was not debating whether salvation was gained by works. No one, including the "men from Judea" who were insisting that the Gentiles become proselytes, believed that anyone gained a place in the world to come by a complete keeping of Torah. Rather, the prevailing view was that a place in the world to come was the gracious gift of God to every Israelite.

Furthermore, if Peter is calling the written Torah an unbearable "yoke," then he is pitting the Scriptures against the true gospel message. But we know Peter did not do this. His message of the gospel given at Pentecost (Shavuot, Acts 2) is based entirely upon the Old Testament. He shows from the Scriptures (Psalms) that the Messiah would suffer and rise from the dead, and that by this work of Messiah the promise of salvation to Israel, as well as to the nations (given in the Abrahamic covenant found in Genesis), would be realized. Far from pitting the Torah against the message of salvation by faith, Peter bases his gospel upon it.

However, Peter is not the only one who affirms the Torah's teaching of salvation by faith. Paul also states that by reading the Torah via the illuminating work of the Spirit, one inevitably sees Jesus.[5] And according to Galatians 3:8, he considers the Abrahamic promise to be the gospel.[6] Moreover, the Apostolic gospel is everywhere grounded in the Old Testament, for these divinely inspired Scriptures provided the apostles' only presentation of the message of salvation.[7]

So if Peter's descriptive phrase "a yoke which neither our fathers nor we have been able to bear" cannot mean the written Torah, then to what was he referring?

James uses similar language in his reference to the requirements given to the Gentiles:

"For it seemed good to the Holy Spirit and to us to lay upon you no greater burden than these essentials..." [8]

Would James have characterized the Torah as a burden? No. In his epistle, written before the Jerusalem Council, James refers to the Torah as "the perfect Torah,"[9] "the Torah of liberty,"[10] and the "royal Torah."[11] Obviously, James considered the Torah an extreme blessing. Apparently both he and Peter had something other than God's Torah in mind when they spoke of the unbearable yoke and a burden.

Yoke and Burden in the Sayings of Jesus

Undoubtedly, Jesus' teachings had remained part of the on-going dialogue among the apostles. Like disciples of any prominent teacher, Jesus' students surely rehearsed His teachings orally before they were written down. It seems certain the oral tradition of His teachings formed the basis for what later become the synoptic Gospels.

Jesus refers to the man-made laws of the Sages via the metaphor of a burden: "And they tie up heavy loads, and lay them on men's shoulders; but they themselves are unwilling to move them with so much as a finger" (Matthew 23:4).

Additionally, He characterizes His own teachings with the familiar term, yoke: "Take My yoke upon you, and learn from Me, for I am gentle and humble in heart; and you shall find rest for your souls. For My yoke is easy, and My load is light" (Matthew 11:29-30).

The use of the term "yoke" in the rabbinic literature is well attested and describes one's willingness to submit to God and His commandments, as well as to the proper interpretation of the Torah and the accepted doctrine of the Sages. As far as the rabbis were concerned, one was not keeping the commandments as he should unless he kept them as prescribed by the ruling authorities—according to the accepted teachings. The "yoke of the commandments" had effectively become the "yoke of the rabbis' interpretations of the commandments," and this yoke was often a burden indeed.

This is why Paul was accused of negating the Torah. It was not God's Torah Paul was negating, but some of the man-made laws that had been added to the Scriptures. In fact, in Acts 21 we read that believing Jews were upset at Paul because the rumor had circulated that he was teaching people to forsake Moses and the customs. So sure were they that he had forsaken God's way they were willing to attempt a mob lynching.

Yet Paul was unwilling to require Gentile believers to submit to the myriad of man-made rabbinical laws in order to be received into the messianic community. And his decision to move in this direction was considered by some to be worthy of death. The "yoke" of tradition had been cast across the neck of Israel for so long that it was impossible for many to envision a genuine faith in God apart from it.

Jesus made a most significant point when He asked His disciples to take upon themselves His yoke, not the yoke of His contemporaries. In contrast to the yoke that the rabbis were laying upon people's shoulders without any intention to help them lighten the load, Jesus identifies His yoke as "easy" (χρηστος, *chrestos*), that is, "kind" and His burden as "light" (ελαφρος, *elaphros*), that is, "not a burden." His yoke was "kind" in that it gave "mercy" and "love" equal significance with "righteousness" and "justice." His burden was "light" because He had unwrapped the teaching of God, the Torah, from all of the man-made extras, and it therefore was able to penetrate the heart with חסד ואמת, *chesed v'emet*, "lovingkindness and truth." Yoked together with Him, the Torah was as sweet as honey and the joy of one's heart. Under this kind and gentle yoke, Jesus intended even the smallest stroke of the Torah and Prophets to be fulfilled in the lives of His followers.[12]

This yoke of the Torah as Jesus taught cannot be the burden and yoke referred to by Peter and James. The yoke they described was unbearable, and even the minimal aspects of it (the four things required of Gentiles) were a burden. Rather, the yoke they were unwilling to place upon the backs of the Gentile believers was the yoke of man-made rules and laws. Indeed, the layer upon layer of rabbinic additions to the Torah had made the whole matter a burden, and had even at times clouded the very purpose of the Torah. The apostles were unwilling to place this burden upon the shoulders of the Gentiles, a burden which the rabbis would have expected every proselyte to bear.

The Four Requirements

Yet there was no way around the fact that the Gentiles would need to conform to some of the man-made laws that for so long had been attached to the Torah. The apostles decreed that an essential group of traditions should be received by the Gentile believers in order to give them a genuine, working membership within the synagogue community.

> "For it seemed good to the Holy Spirit and to us to lay upon you no greater burden than these essentials: that you abstain from things sacrificed to idols and from blood and from things strangled and from fornication; if you keep yourselves free from such things, you will do well. Farewell" (Acts 15:28–29).

Why these four? Is there some commonality that binds them together? Were the Four Requirements really the *Noachide* Laws?

It is not uncommon for scholars to reference the Noachide Laws when discussing the edict drawn up by the Jerusalem Council in Acts 15.[13] Various authors have indicated their belief that the four things required of the Gentiles were a "short list" of the Noachide Laws.

The Babylonian Talmud lists the Noachide Laws as seven:[14] 1) prohibition of idolatry, 2) prohibition of blasphemy, 3) prohibition of bloodshed, 4) prohibition of sexual sins, 5) prohibition of theft, 6) prohibition of eating flesh from a live animal, and 7) requirement to establish a legal system. But to derive these seven from Genesis 1–11 requires reading between the lines.

However, it should be noted that no mention of the Noachide Laws exists in the earliest rabbinic materials. They are a later compilation suited for the time when the synagogue was no longer interested in having Gentiles as part of the community. The formulation of the Noachide Laws thus made a second way for the Gentiles—a way that gave them a place in the world to come without requiring the Jewish community to deal with them.

This renders the Noachide Laws interpretation of Acts 15 unworkable because it is exactly opposite of the council's conclusion. The Jerusalem Council decided that the believing Gentiles were to be received as members of the covenant in exactly the same way as Jews were received—by their faith. What is more, had the Council prescribed the Noachide Laws for the Gentiles, they would have been disobeying Torah. For the Torah itself plainly states that there is one Torah for Israel and the Gentile who dwells with her.

Clearly, the Noachide interpretation does not fit. We must look for another explanation.

The Four Requirements as Fences Against Idol Worship

One thing is clear: The apostles viewed the four requirements given to the Gentile believers as essential. But grouped as they are they comprise a specific message to the Gentiles about a specific issue. Obviously, the apostles were not suggesting to the Gentile believers that all morality and ethical guidelines were summed up in these four. No, an essential issue is described by these four—an issue the apostles knew was a "make-or-break" matter. I would like to suggest that the four prohibitions find a commonality in idol worship in the pagan temples.

From a Jewish perspective, nothing characterized the Gentiles more than idolatry. And nothing was more abhorrent. If Gentiles were allowed into the congregation and community without the requirement of becoming a proselyte, how was the community to be assured that they had made a final break with idolatry? Without the many prohibitions involving touching, handling, eating, etc., how could one be certain the Gentiles, living within the pagan culture, were not participating in the idolatry in which they had been raised?

At this point the Jerusalem Council saw the need for Gentiles to submit to some of the man-made laws. The Jewish community needed to be satisfied that the Gentiles were no longer idolators, and that they had forever turned their backs on this capital crime. In order to make such assurances, the apostles required the Gentile believers to take on the yoke and burden of man-made laws in the area of idolatry.

I suggest that the four items given to the Gentiles are a unified group identifying idol worship in pagan temples. Thus they reveal the apostles' demand that believing Gentiles separate themselves from any contact with the temples that could be construed by the Jewish community as participation in idolatry. In asking the Gentiles to divorce themselves from even the cultural aspects of the pagan temples, the apostles were requiring the Gentiles to view idolatry from the Jewish perspective, and even to conform to some of the additional laws formulated by the Sanhedrin against it. As Ben Witherington writes:

> They must not give Jews in the Diaspora the opportunity to complain that Gentile Christians were still practising idolatry and immorality by going to pagan feasts even after beginning to follow Christ.[15]

Though idolatry would naturally be considered outside the scope of a believer's life, the apostles called for conformity to the additional rabbinic teachings pertaining to idolatry—the "fences" not found in Scripture but necessary in this realm for inclusion into the Jewish community.

When we speak of pagan temples and their rituals, we must remember that in great measure these were seen as cultural and social institutions and not merely as religious ones. For instance, local pagan temples often served as banks for individuals as well as the state, and were the locations for all manner of political issues.[16] Gentiles who had been born and raised in the idolatrous cultures of Greece and Rome had a great many aspects of family and community tied together with the local temples. Could a believing Gentile continue to participate at these temples and even join in political, family, and community events without actually participating in idolatry? Could they eat there without giving their allegiance to the god or goddess to whom the meal was dedicated?

So many daily activities within Roman and Greek society involved the local temple that Gentile believers needed to commit themselves to extra precautions to assure their Jewish brothers that they had forsaken all aspects of idolatry. The four prohibitions listed by the Council were given to do just that.

The Four Prohibitions as Aspects of the Pagan Temple

1 — Abstain from meat offered to idols

The phrase "meat offered to idols" translates only one word in the Greek. This word, ειδωλοθυτος (*eidolothutos*) is used nine times in the New Testament,[17] always in the context of eating food at a pagan temple. This fact is strengthened by the phrase used in the initial listing in Acts 15:20. There "things contaminated by idols" clearly refers to the pollution of food used in rituals of the pagan temple. Likewise, the same word is similarly used in 4Maccabees 5:2. By using this word, the apostles were not prohibiting food from the common market, but specifically food at a ceremonial meal in connection with an idolatrous ceremony.

Thus Gentile believers could not eat a meal in connection with the pagan temples if in any way the food prepared was dedicated to a god or goddess. Of course there were meals and activities in the temple precinct that had nothing to do with the idol housed inside. Apparently these were allowed.

2 — [Abstain from] blood

This does not refer to eating meat with blood—which is discussed in the next prohibition—but to ingesting blood itself, something not uncommon in idol rituals. Whether or not the common person drank the blood of the sacrificial victim is not certain, but there is evidence that the priests did.[18] From a Jewish perspective, to participate in a ritual in which the representative priest drinks the blood of the sacrifice is to participate in the same abominable act. Of course, the Torah prohibits eating blood,[19] but the Apostles required the Gentiles to distance themselves from any ritual in which blood was ingested and/or improperly used. Such a thing was simply too abhorrent for the Jewish community.

3 — [Abstain from] things strangled

The sacrifices in pagan temples were usually killed by cutting the throat. But sometimes they were strangled.[20] This inhumane killing of animals was contrary to the spirit of Torah. While the Torah prohibited eating blood, there is nothing in the written Scriptures describing exactly how an animal was to be slaughtered. In order to fully comply with the Torah commandments against ingesting blood, the Sages felt the necessity to make such rulings. Meat from animals that had been strangled was therefore prohibited because of the high probability that the meat was saturated with blood.

Gentile believers were not to participate in the cruel strangulation of animals nor in the rituals that included such practices. Nor were they to eat the meat of animals that were strangled. As such, meat for sale at the local pagan temple was out of bounds for the Gentile believer. The chances that the meat had been strangled were too high.

4 — [Abstain] from fornication

The word translated "fornication" is πορνεια *(porneia)*, the root of our English word "pornography." While some have suggested that *porneia* here describes prohibited marriages (i.e., too close to the bloodline),[21] the fact is that in Leviticus 18 where prohibited unions are discussed, the LXX *(Septuagint)* never uses the word *porneia*. Granted, *porneia* is used in 1Corinthians 5:1 to describe incest, but that is hardly what the apostles are talking about here.

The word *porneia*, however, is associated with the pagan temple prostitutes.[22] So notorious was temple prostitution in Corinth that the coined phrase "play the Corinthian" meant to engage in sexual promiscuity.[23]

It can hardly be the case, however, that the apostles were speaking of sexual engagement with temple prostitutes when they prohibited "fornication." This would be considered out of the question for all believers and therefore unnecessary to be singled out for Gentiles in particular. Rather, the prohibition is to any connection with the temple rituals that utilized temple prostitutes, including any kind of support or participation in any service that included temple prostitutes, seen or unseen.

In the end, the four prohibitions each attach to an aspect of the pagan temple, and require the believing Gentile to conform to the current teachings of the Jewish community with respect to all matters of idolatry. Their entire separation from the actual idolatry of the pagan temple is emphasized in the final sentence of the edict: *if you keep yourselves free from such things, you will do well.*[24]

The Apostles knew that if the Gentile believers were willing to accept the strict rabbinic teachings regarding all matters of idolatry and particularly regarding the pagan temples, their acceptance within the Torah community would be much greater. Though this could be a burden and at least a part of the yoke of the oral Torah laid upon them, it was essential for their inclusion into the Torah community where they could learn the Scriptures and grow in faith. Their willingness to submit to these additional rulings gave the Jewish community the necessary confidence to receive them as those who had completely forsaken idolatry and turned to the One God of Israel.

Summary

The Jerusalem Council in Acts 15 was dealing with a specific issue: Was it necessary for Gentiles to become proselytes and thus take on the full weight of the man-made laws of the Sages in order to be accepted within the Jewish community. The

Council voiced a unified "no" to this question. Using "circumcision" as a shorthand designation for "the ritual of becoming a proselyte," the Council determined that the Gentiles would not need to be circumcised (i.e., become proselytes) in order to be received into the Torah community.

There was, however, the need to assure the Jewish community that those Gentiles who had confessed Jesus as Messiah had genuinely forsaken any form of idolatry. Since the Greek and Roman cultures were centered around idol worship with local pagan temples, it was important that the Jewish community be able to receive the Gentile believers without any suspicion of remaining idolatry.

The apostles, therefore, required the Gentiles to accept the extra-biblical, man-made laws regarding idolatry. These were:

- They should not participate in any meal that was even remotely connected to idol worship.

- They should not participate in any gathering or ceremony that involved the misuse of blood as a sacrificial element.

- They should not involve themselves in any ritual or ceremony that involved the strangulation of animals, and they should be careful not to eat meat from animals killed through strangulation (something not uncommon in the pagan sacrificial rituals).

- They should distance themselves from any contact with or support of the temple prostitutes and the fornication they represented in the pagan temple precincts.

While the written Torah surely prohibited any worship of idols, the Sages had put a good number of fences in place to distance the people from contact with idolatry. These fences were extra-biblical, yet the apostles considered them essential in showing the clear break the Gentile believers had made with idolatry. But since they were man-made and not directly from Scripture, they were part of the yoke of oral Torah, the burden that the Sages had laid upon the written Scriptures. While the apostles were unwilling to put the Gentiles under the full weight of the traditions—something not even the Jewish people had been able to bear—they did see the need to require the Gentiles to keep this rabbinic teaching. Only such a requirement could have fully satisfied the Jewish community that the Gentile believers had made a radical break from their former idol worship.

Comments and Comparisons of Traditional Christian Theology and Hebraic Thought

1. "If you need proof that the Torah has been done away with, just read Acts 15! Even the Apostles realized it was a heavy burden rather than a gift of God's grace."

Christian interpreters of Acts 15 take the position that the Jews of that day believed their salvation was gained through obedience to the Torah, Peter's statement is interpreted as a ringing declaration against salvation by works. But the Council was not debating whether or not salvation was gained by works. No one, including the "men from Judea", believed that anyone gained a place in the world-to-come by a complete keeping of Torah. Rather, the prevailing view was that a place in the world-to-come was the *gracious gift of God* to every Israelite.

2. "When it comes to Gentile believers, the Apostles instructed them to live according to the Noachide Laws, not the Torah. The Torah is for Jews, the Noachide Laws are for the Gentiles."

Had the Council prescribed the Noachide Laws for the Gentiles, they would have been disobeying Torah. For the Torah itself plainly states that there is one Torah for Israel and the Gentile who dwells with her. (The Noachide laws are of rabbinic, not biblical origin, and were formulated in the later centuries, not in the 1st century.)

3. "Even the Apostles struggled over the issue of the Torah, but Paul finally won. The Jerusalem Council agreed with him that the Torah was not applicable for the Gentile believers."

Peter's message of the gospel given in Acts 2 is based entirely on the Old Testament, confirming the Torah's teaching of salvation by faith. Paul states that by reading the Torah via the illuminating work of the Spirit, one inevitable sees Jesus. James refers to the Torah as "the perfect Torah", "the Torah of liberty", and the "royal Torah." All had something other than God's Torah in mind when they spoke of the unbearable yoke and the burden.

4. "Anyone who says God requires us to live according to Torah hasn't read Acts 15. Even the four things the Apostles required of the Gentiles were cultural, not moral."

As stated before, Acts 15 is referring to man-made laws and not the Torah itself. The Jerusalem Council saw the need for Gentiles to submit to some of those laws. The Jewish community needed to be satisfied that the Gentiles were no longer idolators, and that they had forever turned their backs on this capital crime. In order to make such assurances, the apostles required the Gentile believers to take on the yoke and burden of man-made laws in the area of idolatry in order to give them a genuine, working relationship within the synagogue community. The Apostles knew that the Gentiles coming into the congregations would be learning the Torah more fully as they heard Moses each Sabbath (Acts 15:21).

Study Questions
"Torah is a Burden"

1. What was the primary issue being dealt with at the Jerusalem Council (Acts 15:1–2)?

2. According to the Scriptures, is the Torah a burden to the child of God (Psalm 1:2; 19:7-10; 40:8; 119:77; Romans 7:12-14; James 1:25)? When Jesus spoke of burdens and loads upon people's shoulders, to what was He referring (Matthew 23:1-11; Mark 7: 6-13)? How does this help explain the "burden" referred to in Acts 15:10, 28?

3. Why is it wrong to understand the four requirements of Acts 15 to be the Noachide Laws ? What are the Noachide laws? (Page 37–38)

4. Why did the Jews believe it was necessary for a Gentile to "become a Jew" in order to be saved? What ritual did the 1st century rabbis prescribe for a Gentile who wanted to "become a Jew?" According to Scripture, is it possible for someone to "become a Jew"? What is the only way for a sinner to have forgiveness of sins, according to the Scriptures?

5. What explanation might you give for why the Apostles required the believing Gentiles to adopt the four requirements of the Jerusalem Council (Acts 15)?

When we acknowledge that Torah is God's own self-disclosure to us, we must also recognize the enormous gravity of declaring that same Torah null or void. Even the smallest commandment of the Torah is suffused with Godliness. To declare any commandment as irrelevant or obsolete is to deny the eternal and unchanging nature of God.

Deuteronomy 4:2
Matthew 5:17–19

It is often said

"The Law is Fulfilled"

It is often said, "Those who are telling you that the Torah is for us have failed to understand that Jesus fulfilled the Torah. He said so Himself!" Frequently, when opportunities arise to speak to our family and friends about Torah living, we encounter this line of reasoning. "Since Jesus plainly says that He came to 'fulfill' the Torah, there is no longer any reason for us to concern ourselves with it." It is apparent by this thinking that "fulfill" means "finish" or "complete." Thus, since Jesus "fulfilled" the Torah, He finished it; it's over, nothing more needs to be done in relationship to it.

To strengthen this point of view, the context following Matthew 5:17–20 is interpreted to mean that Jesus speaks of the Torah as deficient. By using the terms "you have heard it said," it is suggested that He sets aside the Torah in favor of His new teaching which He introduces by "but I say:"

> You have heard that the ancients were told, "You shall not commit murder" and "whoever commits murder

shall be liable to the court," but I say to you ... (Matthew 5:21–22)

You have heard that it was said, "You shall not commit adultery," but I say to you ... (Matthew 5:27–28)

Again, you have heard that the ancients were told, "You shall not make false vows, but shall fulfill your vows to the LORD," but I say to you ... (Matthew 5:33–34)

You have heard that it was said, "An eye for an eye, and a tooth for a tooth," but I say to you...(Matthew 5:38–39)

You have heard that it was said, "You shall love your neighbor and hate your enemy," but I say to you ... (Matthew 5:43–44)

When these are read with the preconceived idea that the Torah has been abolished, it appears as though Jesus Himself is teaching against the Torah. But is this really what is being taught here? Was Matthew trying to explain to the Jewish community to whom he wrote that the Messiah Jesus had "fulfilled" the Torah in such a way that it could be set aside so that His followers could advance to a higher level of obedience than their forefathers?

What Does Fulfill Mean in Matthew 5:17?

Some have suggested that Jesus' word "fulfill" was the Hebrew קום (kum); meaning "to establish" or "confirm." This makes sense because of how the word is used in the Old Testament,[1] but also because of how it was used in the Mishnah.[2] It is evident that the verb kum (קום) became a rabbinic favorite to describe the "doing" of Torah commandments. This is important because Mishnaic Hebrew may reflect affinities with the Hebrew and Aramaic spoken in the 1st century.[3] So if Jesus used the word kum when He made His famous statement about "fulfilling" the Torah and the Prophets, then He clearly meant that He came not to set the Torah aside but to establish the Torah, to confirm it, to see that it was carried out or obeyed the way God intended. This, of course, fits with the words of verses 19–20 in which Jesus instructs His disciples to "do" the commandments and teach others to do them as well.

But detractors hasten to point out that the Greek word for "fulfill" in Matthew 5:17 is πληροω (*pleroo*) and that in the Septuagint[4] it never translates the Hebrew word קום (*kum*). In fact, *pleroo* almost always translates another Hebrew word, מלא (*malei*) which means to "be full," "fill up," or "to complete." That Jesus may have used this Hebrew word is strengthened by the fact that the Syriac Peshitta[5] uses the same semitic root *malei* in Matthew 5:17. The Hebrew word *malei* means to "fill up" in the sense of "complete." For example, it is used in the sense of "completing" the set period of time for ritual purification (Leviticus 12:6). The conclusion that many have drawn from this is that Jesus "filled up" the Torah in the sense that He "completed" it. In short, His "fulfilling" of the Torah is understood to mean that it is "finished" and therefore is no longer relevant for us.

Let us suppose that Jesus did use the word *malei* as the Greek and Syriac translations suggest. Is "fulfill" in the sense of "complete" the only meaning of the Hebrew word *malei*? If indeed Jesus used *malei* and not *kum*, what might He have meant?

The Hebrew word *malei* is used in the phrase "to fulfill the words." The setting is that of aging David and the subsequent fight for his throne. Adonijah has declared himself king behind David's back and the prophet Nathan wants Bathsheba to tell David about what has taken place. The prophet says to her:

> Go at once to King David and say to him, "Have you not, my lord, O king, sworn to your maidservant, saying, 'Surely Solomon your son shall be king after me, and he shall sit on my throne'? Why then has Adonijah become king?" Behold, while you are still there speaking with the king, I will come in after you and confirm (*malei*) your words." (IKings 1:13–14)

The phrase translated "confirm your words" uses the Hebrew word *malei* (translated by *pleroo* in the Lxx), the word that usually is translated "fill up" or "complete." But what does it mean to "fill up words?" In the context the meaning is certain: Nathan the prophet "confirms" Bathsheba's words, meaning that he strengthens them and gives them credibility. While she is explaining the situation to King David, Nathan will arrive and confirm that what she has said is true. Since he becomes the second witness, the matter is established. In this case the word *malei* means to "confirm" or "establish" and fits very well with the context of Jesus' statement. His point was that He came to "confirm" the words of the Torah in exactly the same way that Nathan confirmed Bathsheba's words. He came as a witness to establish the Torah's meaning and relevance. In this way He confirms the Torah rather than abolishes it.

Another instance of the word *malei* meaning "confirm" or "establish" is found in Jeremiah 44:25:

> Thus says the Lord of hosts, the God of Israel, as follows: "As for you and your wives, you have spoken with your mouths and fulfilled (*malei*) it with your hands, saying, 'We will certainly perform our vows that we have vowed, to burn sacrifices to the queen of heaven and pour out drink offerings to her.' Go ahead and confirm (*kum*) your vows, and certainly perform your vows!"

Here the confession of the mouth is "fulfilled" (*malei*) with the hands. The point is obvious: what has been said with the mouth is put into action with the hands. This "putting into action" is described by the Hebrew as "fulfilling" what was said. While this verse is in the context of Israel performing idolatry, it still testifies to the fact that the Hebrew word *malei* could be used in the sense of "confirm" or "establish." It links the idea of "fulfilling" (i.e., confirming) with "performing" (i.e., doing).

Jesus also ties these same concepts together in Matthew 5: 17–20. He admonishes His disciples to be great in the Kingdom of God by doing the commandments and teaching others to do them also. This must be seen as an explanation of what He meant by "fulfill" the Torah and the Prophets, in contrast to abolishing them. It hardly seems reasonable that He would have declared an end to the Torah because He had "completed" it and then proceed to admonish His disciples to do the commandments and teach others to do them. The only reasonable interpretation of the passage is that by "fulfill" Jesus meant "to confirm" or "to establish." His point was simply that He came to put the Torah into the lives of the people of God, not to take it away.

The conclusion we reach, then, is that regardless of which of the two Hebrew words Jesus actually spoke, either could bear the meaning required by the context, namely, "to confirm" or "to establish." The argument that the word "fulfill" in Matthew 5:17 must be understood as "finish" or "complete" based upon a possible use of the word *malei* is simply not valid.

'You have heard it said... but I say...'

But what about the second line of reasoning often encountered when discussing Jesus' words in Matthew 5:17–20? In the context immediately following His direct statement of confirming the Torah and Prophets, Jesus goes on to make His point by contrasting what has been heard with what He is saying.

This is often understood to be a contrast between the Torah and the "better way" of Jesus. Indeed, in each of the five contrasts Jesus introduces a quote from the Old Testament with the phrase, "You have heard it said ... "and then contrasts it with His own teaching introduced by, "but I say to you ...." So it is not difficult to understand how people have read this as meaning "this is what you find in the Old Testament ... but I tell you something different" and consequently have come to the conclusion that Jesus considers the Torah now to be replaced by His own teaching.

Most who believe this do not necessarily think the Old Testament is bad. Even in the creeds developed by the ancient Church councils of the 4th and 5th centuries, the Old Testament was received as the inspired and sacred Word of God. Rather, the common position is that Jesus took the Torah to a higher level in His teaching by taking what was only external and making it internal. By this it is meant that Jesus required a higher level of spirituality than the Torah did. To use the Torah as a pattern of righteousness is thus seen to be "going backwards" as far as spirituality is concerned.

Besides the clear emphasis we have already seen in the opening words of Yeshua in verses 17–20, there are two reasons why this traditional approach is wrong. First, a careful reading of the contrasts beginning in verse 21 shows that Jesus includes more than the written Torah when He refers to "You have heard it said..." Secondly, understanding how the phrase, "You have heard it said" was used by rabbis helps us understand what is meant by "you have heard... but I say... ."

The Meaning of "You have heard it said..."

The opposing statements of Jesus that follow His opening teaching on the vitality of the Torah and Prophets are each introduced with the statement "You have heard..." In two of the instances, however, "You have heard..." includes more than a quote from the Old Testament. The phrases, "He who murders shall be liable to the court" (verse 21) and "Love your neighbor and hate your enemy" (verse 43)[6] are not to be found in the Hebrew Scriptures. Nowhere does the Bible commend "hating your enemy."

An interesting parallel to the phrase "you have heard it said" is found in a Jewish teaching on Exodus.[7] Here, in reference to the commandment, "Honor your father and thy mother," the writer says, "I might understand, 'honor them with words only.'" The phrase, "I might understand..." is actually, "I hear..." or "I might hear..." The teaching goes on to refute this proposition and to show that the commandment refers not only to respectful speech but also to the duty of maintaining your parents. Thus, the phrases, "I hear..." or "You hear..." in rabbinic dialog introduces one interpretation of a text, but one with which the writer disagrees.

Daube shows that the early, rabbinical technical terms for "literal meaning" (meaning a "wooden" or "naive" understanding) were שמע (shemua) and משמע (mishma) "that which is heard."[8]

"He who hears..." is used in the sense of "He who sticks to the superficial, literal meaning of Scripture" in the hermeneutical rule according to which "a general summary (like the notice concerning man's creation in the first chapter of Genesis) may be followed by detailed facts (the story of man's creation in the second chapter) which are merely "fleshing out" of what has come before—a repetition giving more particulars. So with this in mind, "He who hears" (who takes Scripture literally, i.e., woodenly[9]) will form the erroneous belief that the second account refers to different facts, but in reality it is merely a repetition with more particulars.[10]

Note in this regard another example from Rabbi Yudah HaNasi in his comments on the phrase "And the LORD came down upon Mount Sinai ...":

> I might hear this as it is heard, (i.e., I might understand this according to its literal meaning). But thou must say: If the sun, one of the many servants of God, may remain in its place and nevertheless be effective beyond it, how much more He by whose word the world came into being.[11]

Here we have the exact same pairing of terms used by Jesus: "heard" and "say." This, then, gives a setting for Jesus' exposition. He is teaching the Torah text, not from a "surface" reading but from a well-informed understanding of the text in light of the whole Torah. "You have heard it said..." introduces a commonly held interpretation but one which Jesus intends to correct by His own understanding of the text, introduced by "but I say to you...." He intends by His teaching to show that one commonly held view of the text is deficient and needs to be reconsidered in light of a fuller understanding of the Torah.

We may therefore conclude that both in the word Jesus used for "fulfill," as well as in His subsequent teaching on specific aspects of the Torah, He wants to point us to the genuine meaning of the Torah. It is not the Torah He calls deficient, but the manner in which it was being commonly taught by some of His contemporaries.

How Does This Apply to Us?

If Jesus was teaching people that the Torah had, to one extent or another, been misunderstood in His day, then it stands to reason that the same might be true in our times. If He was further telling them that the Torah, rightly understood, would provide a light to their path as they purposed to walk with God, then His words speak the same message to us today. The challenge that lies before us is this: Can we read the Torah without placing upon the text the prejudice of nearly 2,000 years? Can we come to the Scriptures seeking to find in them the rich rewards of life God intended for His children? Not only do I hope we can, I am convinced we must.

Comments and Comparisons of Traditional Christian Theology and Hebraic Thought

1. "Don't believe it when you're told the Torah is for today. Jesus fulfilled the Torah, He said so Himself!"

In Matthew 5:17–20 Jesus admonishes His disciples to be great in the Kingdom of God by doing the commandments and teaching others to do them also. This must be seen as an explanation of what He meant by "fulfill" the Torah and the Prophets, in contrast to abolishing them. It hardly seems reasonable that He would have declared an end to the Torah because He had "completed" it and then proceed to admonish His disciples to do the commandments and teach others to do them. The only reasonable interpretation of the passage is that by "fulfill" Jesus meant "to confirm" or "to establish." His point was simply that He came to put the Torah into the lives of the people of God, not to take it away.

2. "The teaching of Jesus goes to a higher level of spirituality than the Torah. If you think the Torah presents a path for righteous living, you're going backwards."

Jesus is teaching the Torah text from a well-informed understanding of the text in light of the whole Torah. "You have heard it said..." introduces a commonly held interpretation but one which Jesus intends to correct by His own understanding of the text, introduced by "but I say to you...." He intends by His teaching to show that one commonly held view of the text is deficient and needs to be reconsidered in light of a fuller understanding of the Torah. Thus He uplifts the Torah to its rightful standing as the way of righteousness.

3. "When Jesus said He had come to fulfill the Torah, He meant He came to finish it. He not only finished it, He also calls His followers to live by a new standard."

Since we now know this issue results from a misunderstanding of the word "fulfill" is it possible that Jesus was teaching people that the Torah had, to one extent or another, been misunderstood in His day? If so, then it stands to reason that the same might be true in our times. If He was further telling them that the Torah, rightly understood, would provide a light to their path as they purposed to walk with God, then His words speak the same message to us today. The challenge that lies before us is this: Can we read the Torah without placing upon the text the prejudice of nearly 2,000 years? Can we come to the Scriptures seeking to find in them the rich rewards of life God intended for His children?

Study Questions
"The Law is Fulfilled"

1. What does the word "fulfill" mean in Matthew 5:17? (Compare the use of the word "confirm" in 1Kings 1:13–14 and the phrase "fulfilled it with your hands" in Jeremiah 44:25). How do the words of Jesus in Matthew 5:18-20 help define His meaning of "fulfill" in v. 17?

2. It is not uncommon to hear people say that the Old Testament dealt with externals, while the New Testament deals with the heart. Why is this a misreading of the Scriptures? (Consider Deuteronomy 4:29, 39; 6:5–6; 7:9; 10:16; 11:13; 2Timothy 3:16.)

3. How was the phrase "You have heard it said... but I say to you" used by the Jewish teachers of Jesus' day?"

4. The Hebrew word "hear" often means "obey." How does Jesus' teaching emphasize this? Matthew 7:21; Luke 6:47–49; 8: 21; John 7:51

5. From a biblical standpoint, what does it mean to truly "hear" the word of the LORD?

6. Jesus said He "did not come to abolish the Torah, but fulfill it." What did He mean by these words?

Endnotes

Chapter 1—"Jesus Broke the Sabbath"

No Endnotes for Chapter 1

Chapter 2—"Torah is a Burden"

1 Acts 15:1, 2.

2 m.*Sanhedrin* 10:1.

3 Cf. also Exodus 12:49 and Numbers 15:29.

4 Acts 15:10, 11.

5 Romans 10:4 where "end" should be understood as "goal." Cf. 2Corinthians 3:1–4:6.

6 Cf. the parallel texts to Genesis 12:3 as well: 18:18; 22:18; 26:4; 27:29; 28:14.

7 Cf. Romans 10:6–8 where Deuteronomy 30:12ff is quoted, and where Paul considers this Torah passage to be "the word of faith which we are preaching." In fact, for Paul Genesis 15:6 —"And Abraham believed God and it was reckoned to him for righteousness"— showed beyond doubt that the message of salvation by grace through faith was the message Abraham believed (cf. Romans 4:3). Paul considers the Abrahamic promise to be the Gospel (Galatians 3:8), the same Gospel he preached.

8 Acts 15:28.

9 James 1:25.

10 James 1:25; 2:12.

11 James 2:8.

12 Matthew 5:17-20.

13 Brad H. Young, *Paul the Jewish Theologian* (Hendrickson, 1997), 38ff; Marvin Wilson, *Our Father Abraham* (Eerdmans, 1989), 49; W. D. Davies, *Paul and Rabbinic Judaism*, 3rd edition (SPCK, 1970), 118; Mark Nanos, *The Mystery of Romans* (Fortress, 1996), 169–170; Alan Segal, *Paul the Convert* (Yale, 1990), 194ff.

14 b.*Sanhedrin* 56a-60a; b.Avoda Zara 64b.

15 Ben Witherington, *The Acts of the Apostles*, (Eerdmans, 1998) 463.

16 J. R. C. Cousland, "Temples, Greco-Roman" in Evans and Porter, eds., *Dictionary of New Testament Background* (IVP, 2000), 1186.

17 Acts 15:29; 21:25; 1Corinthians 8:1, 4, 7, 10; 10:19; Revelation 2:14, 20.

18 R. M. Oglivie, *The Romans and Their Gods in the Age of Augustus* (New York, 1969), 49ff.

19 Leviticus 3:17; 17:12.

20 See the magical papyri PGM XII.14–95, "Take also on the first day seven living creatures and strangle them; one cock, a partridge, a wren... Do not make a burnt offering of any of these; instead, taking them in your hand strangle them, while holding them up to your Eros, until each of the creatures is suffocated and their breath enters him. After that place the strangled creatures on the altar together with aromatic plants of every variety." Quoted from Witherington, Acts, 464 n.423. Interestingly, even Philo mentions that some were sacrificing animals by means of strangulation: Philo, *The Special Laws*, iv:xiii.122.

21 Cf. W. K. Lowther Clarke, *New Testament Problems* (Macmillan, 1929), 59–60; F. F. Bruce, *The Acts of the Apostles* (Eerdmans, 1951), 300.

22 Hauch/Schultz, "πορνεια" in *TDNT*, 6:581f, though with regard to πορνεια in Acts 15 the authors come to the conclusion that it refers to prohibited marriages.

23 C. S. Keener, "Adultery, Divorce" in Evans and Porter, eds., *Dictionary of New Testament Background* (IVP, 2000), 12.

24 Acts 15:29.

Chapter 3—"The Law is Fulfilled"

1 The hifil of קום is used in the Old Testament of "confirming" covenants: Genesis 6:18; 9: 9, 11; 17:7, 19; Exodus 6:4; Leviticus 26:9; Deuteronomy 8:18; 2 Kings 23:3; Jeremiah 34: 18; Ezekiel 16:60, 62.

2 Note that קום can mean "to sustain" or "maintain" the teaching of a Sage, m.*Gittin* 3:4; and in the Talmud קום is used as "fulfilling, maintaining, carrying out, or executing" the whole Torah, b.*Yoma* 28b. For a full listing cf. Jastrow, *Dictionary of the Talmud* (חרוב, n.d.), 1330.

3 Bruce K. Waltke and M. O'Connor, *An Introduction to Biblical Hebrew Syntax* (Eisenbrauns, 1990), p. 10. Interestingly, the translation of the New Testament into Modern Hebrew uses קום *(kum)* to translate Jesus' word "fulfill," reflecting late common usage in rabbinic Hebrew.

4 The Septuagint is the Greek translation of the Old Testament, often called the Lxx.

5 The Syriac translation of the Old Testamen and the New Testamen completed by the 3rd century B.C.

6 The first edition of the *NASB* puts the phrase "and hate your enemy" in small caps to show that it is a quote from the Old Testamen, but this is an error.

7 *Mekhilta* on Exodus 19:20.

8 Daube, *The New Testament and Rabbinic Judaism* (London: School of Oriental and African Studies, 1956), 56.

9 The parenthesis is my explanatory addition.

10 Daube, Op. Cit., p. 56. This is from the 32 principles of interpretation of Eliezer ben Yose HaGelili. These are listed and expounded in R. Adin Steinsaltz, *The Talmud: A Reference Guide* (Random House, 1989), 147–154. The principle alluded to here is number 13.

11 *Mekhilta* on Exodus 19:20.

1-800-4-YESHUA

Hebraic & Messianic Resources Catalog

We are honored to present a catalog of books, teaching resources, and materials that will connect you with the roots of your faith which are found in the Land, the People and the Scriptures of Israel.

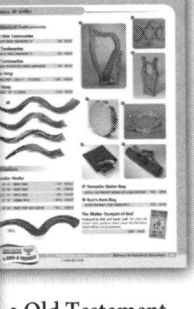

- Messianic Thought and History
- New Testament Backgrounds
- Old Testament Backgrounds
- Messianic Lifestyle
- God's Appointed Times
- Traditional Jewish Thought

- Bibles
- Messianic Music
- Hebrew Learning
- Judaica & Gift items

Our name is our mission. Everything that we are and do is to glorify the Name of the Messiah and bring praise to Him.

In naming this catalog **1-800-4-YESHUA** we are burdened to operate at the highest level of customer service, integrity, and professionalism.

1-800-4-YESHUA is dedicated to:
- Excellent Customer Service
- Fast Shipping and Order Processing
- Competitive Pricing and Quality Products

Request your free catalog, call *1-800-775-4807*

REQUEST EXTRA CATALOGS FOR FRIENDS

 First Fruits of Zion